Books of related interest by Sam Hamill

Wen Fu: The Art of Writing
          (from the Chinese of Lu Chi)

Banished Immortal: Visions of Li T'ai-po

Facing the Snow: Visions of Tu Fu

Bashō's Ghost
          (essays)

A Poet's Work: The Other Side of Poetry
          (essays)

A Dragon in the Clouds

A Dragon
in the Clouds

poems and

translations by

Sam Hamill

Broken Moon Press

Printed in the United States of America.

ISBN 0-913089-11-7

Library of Congress Catalog Card Number: 89-61141

Cover painting, *Bird Experiencing Light,* by Morris Graves.
  Used by permission of the artist and The Seattle Art Museum,
  Eugene Fuller Memorial Collection, 70.16.

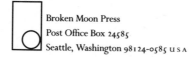

Broken Moon Press
Post Office Box 24585
Seattle, Washington 98124-0585 USA

*To my friend, Jaan Kaplinski
and to my daughter, Eron Hamill*

CONTENTS

❖ Visions of Ryōkan

❖ *Figures on a Shoji Screen*

❖ *Tangled Hair*

Acknowledgments

The author would like to express his gratitude to the Japan-U.S. Friendship Commission, the U.S. National Endowment for the Arts, and the Japanese Agency for Cultural Affairs (Bunka-chō) for a Japan-U.S. Fellowship during 1987–88. There is little doubt that without their support much of the work herein would never have come to fruition.

A Dragon in the Clouds

Homework

❖ *Prolegomenon:*
Three Ages, Three Worlds

We live in all Three Ages:
the past we carry with us;

the present we inhabit;
each step: into the future.

The Three Worlds and its postures?—
formlessness comes soon enough;

form is the transient body;
all the rest is desire, Love.

All the quiet afternoon splitting wood,
thinking about books, I remembered

Snyder making a handle for an ax
as he remembered Ezra Pound,

thirty years before,
thinking about Lu Chi.

Using the ax, I forget the ax.
Closing my eyes, I see.

This morning at sunrise, I heard
the first finch of the new year.

Last night, Tree found a spider
large as her thumb in her room.

A housefly buzzes against the window,
angry to get out.

Outside, the ping, ping of a bumblebee
banging to get in.

When the last spring rain
strips the rhododendrons

and petals lie scattered at their roots
bleaching slowly in the sun, turning white,

I sit alone through the long afternoon,
warm breeze blowing through me,

a whisper of distant bees,
green world bathed with infinite light.

Sun warm on my back like your hands,
Coltrane blowing "Soul Eyes" and "Nancy"—

tulips almost black rising to meet
the last pale blossoms on the weeping cherry:

a few lines of music, a word, a flower,
recover a sweetness I'd lost.

In the garden, a deluge of stones, motionless,
between two hills of deep green moss.

Thirty-one new yellow daffodils
bloom in the little garden.

Alder seed covers everything
with little flakes of rust.

A breeze through evergreens.
Distant bird-trills.

When Hui Neng tore up the Sutras,
his bones were already dust.

When evening comes,
her kisses are cool and wet.

I washed my clothes and dishes
and finally made the bed.

Winter arrives with cold hands and hunger.
Autumn drops yellow calling cards and goes.

Fourth night, the same pot of stew.
No stars. The rain continues.

Under the cold blue quarter moon,
Jupiter and Mars ride low

deep in the west over mountains
December snow has frosted.

No one to talk with, no one around,
I try sitting zazen, eyes closed,

but still see only you:
the thousand arms of Kannon.

On such a clear warm night, how can I not think
of Li Po searching for the moon in the river,

a little too drunk to believe
any old thing could matter?

It isn't true he drowned
embracing the moon's reflection:

no one but a monkey
would look for the moon in water.

Coming home late to an empty house,
tired, I doze off in my chair.

Rain falls on the roof
soft as your hair on my face.

The woodstove sighs and sizzles,
a whisper in the night.

Like Chuang Tzu, I know I am dreaming,
but hope I will never wake.

Wanting one good organic line,
I wrote a thousand sonnets.

Wanting a little peace,
I folded a thousand cranes.

Every discipline a new evasion;
every crane a dodge:

Bashō didn't know a thing about water
until he heard the frog.

Tu Fu eased his heavy heart
by composing accurate couplets.

Li Po relied on wine
and the moon's inspiration.

Fifteen hundred years
have vanished in a moment,

and here we are, still brooding
on the uselessness of letters.

❖ Note Pinned to a Tree

No one home this afternoon.
Enjoy the woodsmoke in the air.

This garden's as well-tended
as any you're likely to find.

I waited just long enough to watch
a huge cloud pass, silent as a schooner.

No one home. Old work clothes,
newly washed, luff along the line.

A Dragon

in the Clouds

❖ *Black Marsh Eclogue*

Although it is midsummer, the great blue heron
holds darkest winter in his hunched shoulders,
those blue-turning-gray clouds
rising over him like a storm from the Pacific.

He stands in the black marsh
more monument than bird, a wizened prophet
returned from a vanished mythology.
He watches the hearts of things

and does not move or speak. But when
at last he flies, his great wings
cover the darkening sky, and slowly,
as though praying, he lifts, almost motionless,

as he pushes the world away.

❖ *Moon Watching Pavilion*

I.

Two weeks ago, when daffodils were freshly bloomed
into huge, yellow blossoms, I stood with you
out on the Moon Watching Pavilion
at the far end of our Japanese garden,

full moon pillowed in clouds,
flowers so pale in moonlight they seemed
almost memory, more dream than substance.
I knew it wasn't right, but I wanted to nail

the moon right there in the sky, a huge zero
high above our house drowning in a pool
of smoky clouds. Now it is May, and truly spring,
white blossoms on plum trees,

weeping cherry lavender with buds,
pink flowers on wild currants, tulips
purple—almost black before they open.
Two rusty robins farm the edge of the garden.

II.

In early May, mid-day, I take my zafu
out to sit on the Pavilion.
The *Koshoji* says outward attachment to form
results in inward confusion, "contact

with circumstances itself creates confusion."
All I can hear in the quiet afternoon
are a few gulls far out over the water
searching for the end of the sky,

a crow somewhere nearby, constantly chuckling.
I hear myself breathe a few moments, and then
it passes like a shadow. The gray cotton sky disappears.
"The flesh is the body, home to three Buddhas."

What use is *Kabbalah* or the Sutras?
In a week, a new moon emerges.
Yugen, the mystery. The body is a temple,
not a refuge. *Mahaprajnaparamita.*

❖ *Tammuz in the Garden*

Stretched naked in the sunlit garden,
how can I not name the flowers
blooming one by one,

how can I not think of lovely Helen
when she was still a goddess,
kidnapped as she picked

from a small garden such as this
a small bouquet, her loveliness,
her innocence

taken by violence and lust.
But the garden does not judge.
It rises in its season

as evidence of being—
the soil in the hand is the flesh
becoming—

the garden blooming is the brief
declarative sentence,
seed syllable

from the heart of great silence.

❖ *A Dragon in the Clouds*

It is solstice,—
hot, dry,
air too heavy to move,
the mountains hazy blue.

I have been baking in the sun
with Euripides' fable of Helen.

And now, quietly,
a finch has flown down from the cedar
to perch on the window sill.

And I realize
she is curious,
she is watching,

and has cautiously stepped closer.

The beauty of the tragic,
the tragedy of the lovely,

she doesn't know or care to remember.

She knows two things:
the world is flat,
and that she lives

on this side
of the only river
she cannot fly across.

She looks at emeralds
in the grass and sees
only common seed.

And now she has come closer
once again,

her head cocked,
surveying my naked body.

Her eyes are large
and wearied by their knowledge,

like Kawabata's eyes
which knew
only sadness and beauty.

I close my book very slowly,
lay my head on my arms,
and look her in the eye:

she has become my lover
and my Dharma Master.

Morris Graves says birds
inhabit a world without karma.

❖ A Warbler's Song in the Dusk

I crossed an ocean
dappled by high drifting clouds
blown on winter winds
to hear the warbler's solo
stir old memories of my vows.

———

Little Japanese
uguisu, little warbler
singing in the dusk,
do you remember lovers,
is that why you sing for us?

———

The plum blossoms fall,
soon the cherry trees will bud.
Someone plays piano
in a house not far away.
And your sad soprano calls.

———

A car on the road,
the noise of growing cities—
even one small bird
returns the human spirit
to ancient joys and pities.

———

Millions of people
in cars and trains and subways
buy and sell and trade—
one lonely warbler singing,
and we give our hearts away.

———

Uguisu, your song
and your name are the same.
A moment alone—
listen to your song, it's true,—
and the soul sings out again.

———

❖ *Watching the Waves*

For fifty years I've drifted,
carried on wandering waves
like a single grain of sand
from a beach a world away.

Yun-men raised his dragon staff:
it swallowed earth and heaven.
Gills and scales at Dragon Gate,
all these years chasing waves!

You return to your cottage
nestled in northern mountains.
I remain in the city,
red dust burning in my eyes.

Moonlight troubles the waters;
mountains and rivers remain.
Blinding light every morning;
in the evening, clouds and rain.

❖ The Uta Mound

Dusk, the Omi Sea,
a lone plover skimming waves,
and with each soft cry
my heart too, like dwarf bamboo,
stirred, longing for bygone days.
        —KAKINOMOTO NO HITOMARO

Ruined capitals
at Omi and Yoshino
long since turned to dust.
Sunlight sets fields ablaze
in cold eastern dawn;
facing west, the moon returns
to its hilltop grave.
He who walked the Aki fields
knows eternal rest
deep within the Uta Mound,
ancient Yamato
protected by wide mountains,
Fujiwara gods,
and by Hitomaro's songs.

The Empress Jitō
still haunts Yoshino fields,
a pale, aging ghost
mourning her husband and son,
wandering mountains
and slow crystalline rivers
where her palace stood,
boats on the morning water
strewn with spring blossoms,
cormorants fishing shallows
wrapped in mists of time.
No more than a dream remains—
the Empress, the song
from a time no one can know.

When he left his wife
at Tsuno Cove in Iwami,
winds took morning wings
and the waves took evening wings
singing in his ears
like thunder throwing offing;
and at Cape Kara
on the Sea of Iwami,
the sway of seaweed
like the sway of love he longed
to feel in his arms
again, Hitomaro rode

to the capital
alone with the lonely moon.

At Sento-Gosho,
beyond Omiya Palace
and Akose Pool,
the rockery, Tosa Bridge,
islands in the pond
where royalty strolled and dreamed—
at Sento-Gosho,
just beyond the gray stone shore
of South Pond's Dreary Beach,
beyond Seikatei Teahouse,
the poet's shrine: small,
quiet. Almost no one comes.
Just a man in sum.
But among *Man'yoshu* poets,

almost a god, a sovereign.

Sedoka

Kakinomoto
no Hitomaro, poet.
Nothing to learn of the man.
Dusty worn old shrine.
He walks in *komoriku,*
he wanders the hidden land.

❖ Ten Thousand Buddhas

for Seki Kazuo

The first pale light
silhouettes the mountains.

All along the valley's rising hills,
deep woods of gray hannoki alder

begin to bud, a few crows
clucking in their branches.

Beyond the trees,
the river sings.

Countless shallow pools
reflect the empty morning sky

where, last night,
thousands of moons were shining.

Somewhere, a farm wife
begins her family's breakfast.

Men who work the stone-crushing plant
rise, pull on overalls, yawn,

and greet the day.
The world is difficult, but good.

From the woods, a faint *bup-pō-so,*
bup-pō-so, song of the Buddha-bird.

And once again,
the frogs begin their sutra.

———

That's not Mount Sumeru, snowy cold,
defining the horizon. These forests

are no man's arana—groves
of a yogin's retreat.

Pitched against this sky, Mount Sumon
towers over valleys

children call Mole and Wasabi,
over mirrored rice fields,

rising like a dream, like a phantom,
like any mountain seen

by a man with a broken begging bowl
two hundred years ago

or five hundred years before that:
Ryōkan or Kamo no Chomei

might live there in a hut;
Bashō might wear it like a hat.

What's any mountain but a signpost
along a wanderer's route?

A thousand fields in a thousand valleys
like the thousand arms of Kannon.

Ten thousand mountains over ten thousand fields
with rice shoots to be planted—

the dew of the world, the bent back.
The fields soak. The soil is rich black.

❖ *Yung-chia Reconsidered*

A wind in the pines,
moonlight trembling on the stream
at deepest midnight
on the coldest evening:
what does it mean.

❖ *Organic Form*

A year on one line,
searching for the poetry:
outside, breezes rise—
spring to summer to autumn—
leaves fall, rot, and feed the tree.

❖ *Hakutsu's Pine*

A great pine stands close
by the old stone house.
Examine it in detail:
like meeting ancient sages
face-to-face.

Visions

of Ryōkan

Ryōkan, if
anyone should ask, had
these last words for the world:
Namu Amida Butsu—
and offered nothing more.

No bird above these wild hills.
Garden leaves fall one by one.

Desolate autumn winds:
a man alone in thin black robes.

Dawn, the shrine under silver snow,
trees flower white on the grounds.

Out in the cold, one small boy
throwing snowballs—all the world his own.

❖ *Reply to a Friend*

Too stupid to live among men,
I pass my years among herbs and trees;

too lazy to learn right from wrong,
laugh at me, and I laugh along.

These old bones still cross the river,
begging-bag in hand, loving springtime weather.

I manage to survive.
I never once despised this world.

Nothing satisfies some appetites,
but wild plants ease my hunger.

Free of untoward desires,
all things bring me pleasure.

Tattered robes warm frozen bones.
I wander with deer for companions.

I sing to myself like a crazy man,
and children sing along.

I never longed for the wilder side of life.
Rivers and mountains were my friends.

Clouds consumed my shadow where I roamed,
and birds pass high above my resting place.

Straw sandals in snowy villages,
a walking stick in spring,

I sought a timeless truth: the flowers' glory
is just another form of dust.

South sea floors are home to coral reefs,
lupine flourishes in arctic mountains.

On all this earth, each thing has a home
determined as a birthright.

I left my home in my green years
to wander a thousand miles.

I visited the huts of aging masters
to suffer their discipline.

Wanting a way for my own good faith,
I never indulged in the flesh.

Now like a dream the years are gone
and I am weathered with age.

Near my hut on the mountain,
I gather sprouts of bracken.

Young, I sat long hours of zazen
to master each quiet breath.

Snows and stars were my texts,
hunger and sleep unnoticed.

What peace my heart knows now
I owe to the discipline of youth. Yes, seek.

But lacking the artless art, each lesson
learned but once, who am I to preach?

❖ *New Year Poem*

Life bolts like a horse through a gate.
Year by year, we pile debts we've wrangled.

Tomorrow begins another year
and I'm already grizzled and bedraggled.

The river willows wave their arms,
plums perfume the mountains.

I haven't wings to fly against the storm,
but like a phoenix, lift my voice to sing.

I know a gentleman poet
who writes in the high old way—
master of form from Han and Wei
or new-style modeled on the T'ang.

With elegant strokes, he quietly composes,
deftly adding images to startle.
He hasn't learned to speak from the heart:
all wasted! Though he writes all night long.

As a boy, I studied literature
but failed to become a scholar.

I sat for years in zazen,
but failed my Dharma Master.

Now I inhabit a hut
inside a Shinto shrine:

half common custodian,
half prophet of the Buddha.

Sixty years a poor recluse alone
in a hut near a cliffside shrine.

Night rains fall and carve the cliff.
On the sill, my candle sputters in the wind.

The winds have died, but flowers go on falling;
birds call, but silence penetrates each song.

The Mystery! Unknowable, unlearnable.
The virtue of Kannon.

Lugging firewood down from the summit,
the winding trail is never easy.

Rest awhile under red pines
where spring birds are singing.

Illusion and enlightenment are mutually entangled:
means and end, cause and effect are one.

Dawn to dusk, I study wordless texts in silence;
nights are lost to thoughtless meditation.

Warblers sing in the willows,
dogs bark in the moonlit village.

All emotions rise in a whirl.
I leave this old heart to the world.

You stop to point at the moon in the sky,
but the finger's blind unless the moon is shining.

One moon, one careless finger pointing—
are these two things or one?

The question is a pointer guiding
a novice from ignorance thick as fog.

Look deeper. The mystery calls and calls:
no moon, no finger—nothing there at all.

His cane he carved from rabbit-horn,
his robes he wove from air.

His sandals came from tortoise-wool.
He sang his poems with silent mouth

so everyone could hear.

Figures

on a Shoji Screen

All this summer night
I thought of going to bed.
Now, with a single note
from the cuckoo,
daybreak.

TSURAYUKI
(883–946)

Weary clear to his feet,
the cuckoo hiding
in the mountains—
does he still sing
even when no ones listens?

FUJIWARA NO SANEKATA
(d. 998)

Late evening finally comes:
I unlatch the door
and quietly await
the one
who greets me in my dreams.
            YAKAMOCHI
            (718–785)

Early morning glows
in the faint shimmer
of first light.
Choked with sadness,
I help you into your clothes.
            ANONYMOUS
            (*Kokinshu* 637)

In the dark godless month,
alone with rain,
myself my only companion,
a dark trail into the mountains:
I climb into my sadness.

THE MONK SOSEI
(ca. 890)

Even when we wandered together,
the mountain in autumn
was almost impossible to cross.
How can you even hope
to make that journey alone?

PRINCESS OKU
(7th C.)

River fog rises,
burying the foothills:
the autumn mountain
hangs
from a nail in the sky.

KIYOWARA FUKUYABU
(900–930)

Under the sky's broad reaches,
like ice
almost imperceptibly melting,
may your heart
melt for me.

ANONYMOUS
(*Kokinshu* 542)

Across Kasuga Moor,
like early morning clouds
gathering, slowly gathering,
my love increases
through all these empty hours.

OTOMA NO KATAMI
(ca. 750)

Like a tall ship
rocking at anchor
in its final port-of-call,
love exhausts me:
endless memories your name recalls.

PRINCE YUKE
(7th C.)

In the autumn sea,
the moon lifts and falls
on waves
trying to wash it away:
only its beauty remains.

KIYOWARA FUKUYABU
(900–930)

Angry river winds
grow bitter cold, so cold
this long winter's night
going to see my love
even the plovers cry.

TSURAYUKI
(883–946)

Light snow silently sweeps
the little garden
through this long cold night.
Without your arm for a pillow,
how can I hope to sleep?

YAKAMOCHI

(718–785)

Little nightingale,
if you refused to sing,
how would those who live
in mountain village snow
recognize the spring?

NAKATSUKASA

(ca. 900)

Spending the whole night
neither awake nor asleep,
then the whole day spent
ruminating over rain—
the torrents of spring never end.

ARIWARA NO NARIHIRA
(825–880)

Where is the dark seed
which grows the forget-you-plant?
Searching, now I see
it grows only in the heart
of one who has murdered love.

THE MONK SOSEI
(ca. 890)

How very much love I gave!
If you must know
a number,
go to the shore at Tago,
try to count the waves.

FUJIWARA NO OKIKAZE
(ca. 910)

My love grows
like numberless grasses
deep within the mountains:
their amplitude increases
though no one comes to count them.

ONO NO YOSHIKI
(d. 902)

Like an old love-letter
scrawled across
a worn slate sky
in watery ink:
wild geese return.

TSUMORI KUNIMOTO
(1023–1103)

All alone
beside the temple bell:
I stole away
to meet you here.
Now the fog has cleared.

YOSANO AKIKO
(ca. 1900)

Men love to gossip,
and their every word is mean.
Now it comes to this:
at dawn I cross the river,
never again to be seen.

> PRINCESS TAJIMA
> (ca. 687)

The fall moon still shines
as it did when you were here.
But you who lit my days—
gone. I watch alone
as the years drift on and on.

> KAKINOMOTO NO HITOMARO
> (ca. 692)

Tangled Hair

❖ *Socho's Song Considered*

hito no nasake ya
ana ni aruran

People concentrate
All emotions on a hole.

❖ *Midaregami*

Reading Yosano Akiko's *Tangled Hair*
I find you everywhere:

In moonlight and rain, in her lotus dew,
in Akiko's tangled hair.

All those ancient tragedies
and comedies in every little tune—

Sapphic. Catullan.
In every poem, you.

❖ *Dolphin Song*

Your hands on my body
bring dreams of summer gardens,

islands with white beaches
where dolphins swim.

I drift under your fingers
like a shadow under water.

Whenever you touch me,
my whole body glistens.

❖ *Song of the Dream Garden*

—I<small>KKYŪ</small>

Pillowed on your thighs in a dream garden,
little flower with its perfumed stamen,

singing, sipping from the stream of you—
sunset; moonlight; our song continues.

❖ *Mountains and Rivers without End*

After making love, we are like
rivers come down from mountain summits.

We are still, we are moving,
calm in the depths of danger—

two rivers entering the sea
slowly, as if nothing matters:

quietly, but with great power,
merging in deepening waters.

❖ *Pianissimo*

Lying here beside you, your breath slow,
deep, and growing deeper on tides of dream,

your skin cool, moist with lovesweat and
my fingers riding the long road of your body

into groves, hills, and plains, riding
the rivers of your eyes, falling like light

across your face into utter darkness,
that complete silence which embraces . . .

❖ *After Clouds and Rain*

It rained all day. Now a single bird
sings madly in the forest.

I like to think of your body wet
and smelling of bubblebath.

The little bird chuckles, laughs,
then waits a few moments in silence.

You comb out your soaking hair.
Raindrops trickle through leaves.

❖ *Fire and Water*

After you bathed
and powdered
and went away:

your cool wet towel
against my burning face

❖ *Awkward Waltz*

You wanted to be
a moon, a star.

Now I watch the cold
blank empty heavens

burning on alone,
like you,

so far
from where you are.

I've read your letter
so many times I've
got it memorized—
that voice—What's better?
Laughter in your eyes.

I don't know a thing
about satori—
"enlightenment" is boring.
Together, let's undress.
Honor the dharma of the flesh.

❖ *By Example*

Hui Kuo's devotion
to Bodhidharma
lead him to cut off
his good left arm. What,
Love, shall I remove for you?

❖ Ten Thousand Sutras

after Hakuin's Meditation Sutra

The body is the body of the Buddha.
Like ice and water, the one is always in the other.

In the middle of the lake
we long for a drink of water.

Adrift in Samsara
we dream of blissful Nirvana.

This body is the body of the Buddha,
this moment an eternity.

Saying *I love you,* the deed is done—
the name and the deed are one.

With you and without you
the line runs straight—

your body is the body of the Buddha,
there is light beyond the gate.

This love I give to you
is the love that comes from Kannon.

Every breath a sutra.
Going or returning, it's the same.

Our bodies are the bodies of the Buddha,
our names are Kannon's name.

No word can adequately say it,
yet every word must praise it—

in silent meditation
destroying evil karma,

in silent meditation
inhabiting the Dharma—

this body is the body of the Buddha,
your body is the body of the Buddha.

Open arms and eyes to Samsara!
Embraced by the thousand arms of Kannon!

In the perfect mind of vivikta-dharma,
the truth of solitude,

our body is a temple,
not a refuge.

Praise our body
even in Samsara,

our bodies are the body of the Buddha,
our bodies are the body of the Buddha.

❖ *Kannon*

I adore you. I love you
completely. Nothing to ask in return.

Each act of affection a lesson:
I fail, but with each failure, learn.

Like studying
under Te-shan:

thirty blows if I can't answer,
thirty blows if I can.

❖ Notes on the Poems

HOMEWORK

These poems grew out of journal entries written in a verse form which loosely parallels the eight-line classical Chinese *lu-shih* (regulated verse) without insistence upon the syllabic count, rhyme scheme, or strict syntactical parallelism of the original.

Page 6: All the quiet afternoon: See Gary Snyder's *Axe Handles* and Ezra Pound's comments on the *Wen Fu* of Lu Chi, as well as my own translation of this great third-century *Art of Writing*.

Page 8: When the last spring rain: Last line: "Infinite Light" is the meaning of the name Amida Buddha.

Page 10: Thirty-one new yellow daffodils: Hui Neng (the Sixth Patriarch) teaches that zazen is the result rather than the cause of enlightenment. In *The Platform Sutra* he demolishes Buddhist dogma: "The profound meaning of all the Buddhas has no connection to words and letters!" And "Buddha-nature is non-dualism." He demonstrated his enlightenment by burning the Sutras.

Page 12: Under the cold blue quarter moon: Kannon (*Kuan Shih Yin* in Chinese) is the Bodhisattva of Compassion; in Sanskrit, *Avalokitesvara*. In Japan, Kannon is often seen in a masculine incarnation as at the great Kiyomizudera (Clear Water Temple) in Kyoto; in China, most often in a feminine incarnation holding a vase from which she "pours the morning dew," and in one incarnation is "eleven-headed, thousand-armed."

Page 13: On such a clear warm night: A famous myth claims that Li T'ai-po drowned trying to embrace the reflection of the moon in the Yellow River. The myth was probably drawn from an episode in the *Mahaparanirvana Sutra* in which Monkey does the same thing.

Page 14: Coming home: See the famous episode in *Chuang Tzu* about the Master and the butterfly (especially Burton Watson's translation from Columbia University Press).

Page 15: Wanting one good organic line: Folding paper cranes as a gesture inviting peace is an ancient Japanese tradition.

A DRAGON IN THE CLOUDS

Page 22: Moon Watching Pavilion: *Mahaprajnaparamita:* "The perfection of wisdom."

Page 26: A Dragon in the Clouds: The idea of birds inhabiting a karma-free world goes back to before Zen; but the idea was first brought to my attention by Morris Graves in Ray Kass's study of his work, *Visions of the Inner Eye* (George Braziller, Inc., 1983).

Page 31: Watching the Waves: See koan 60 in *The Blue Cliff Record*. See also Ikkyū Sōjun's poem, "Peach Blossom Waves," in *The Crazy Cloud Anthology*. This poem is for Keida Yusuke.

Page 32: The Uta Mound: See Kakinomoto no Hitomaro's *choka* (longer poems) and *waka* (shorter poems) in the *Man'yoshu.* The "Uta Mound" is his shrine at Sento-Gosho, the "former emperor's palace" in Kyoto. The poem follows the structure of his choka, with a *sedoka* rather than waka for an envoy.

Page 38: Yung-chia Reconsidered: Yung Chia (d. 713), early Zen master and author of *Cheng Tao Ke.* After "reconsidering" his Chinese quatrain, I recast it in the form of a waka; later, the Japanese poet Keida Yusuke and I reconsidered it once again, this time in the form of a haiku [*Matsu-kaze ya/ kawamo ni yureru/ yowa-no-tsuki,* "A wind in the pines—/ on the river's face/ the moon trembles"]. Originally presented as a koan, the poem continues to present its koan in all three forms and languages some 1200 years later.

Page 40: Hakutsu's Pine: From the Japanese Zen monk (ca. 704).

Visions of Ryōkan

Ryōkan (1758-1831) was a reclusive Buddhist monk of the Soto branch of Zen whose religious name means "Goodly Tolerance," and who also referred to himself as *Daigu* or "Great Fool." He lived for years in a one-room hut on Mt. Kugami near Niigata in northwest Honshu, studying his beloved *Man'yoshu* along with the poems of Kanzan (Cold Mountain), Su Tung-p'o, and the twelfth-century Zen monk Saigyo. He extolled the virtues of reciting the *Nembutsu* and believed devoutly in the Western Paradise of the Shin sect. He also loved playing games with children. His poverty was not feigned: he didn't even receive the "five measures of rice" for which his hermitage, Gogo-an, was named. He wrote many poems, in Chinese and in Japanese, some of which are still being discovered. My versions are based on his *kanshi* (poems written in Chinese). Burton Watson's 1977 volume, *Ryōkan: Zen Monk-Poet of Japan,* is brilliant. Also recommended: John Stevens's *One Robe, One Bowl.* There are prose renderings by Nobuyuki Yuasa, *The Zen Poems of Ryōkan.* This suite is dedicated to Burton Watson, whose books have nourished and inspired me for a quarter-century. Nine bows.

Page 43: Ryōkan, if: The invocation of Amida Buddha's name, *Namu Amida Butsu.*

Page 53: As a boy, I studied literature: Ryōkan spent his last days as a caretaker at a Shinto shrine in Niigata Prefecture.

Page 55: The winds have died: Kannon (see page 12 note, above).

Figures on a Shoji Screen

These poems are drawn mostly from the *Kokinshu,* the great tenth-century Japanese anthology, with a few from the earlier *Man'yoshu.* I have arranged these poems into parallel "conversations" between two imaginary lovers, the "figures" on the screen.

The title is from Yosano Akiko's incandescent erotic tanka, *Midaregami*, published in 1901, a book which inspired many of these brief lyrics. Extant translations are, alas, barely adequate. The desire to be free of desire is an arrogant desire. Asked for a demonstration of his zen, one old master replied, "When hungry, I eat; when thirsty, I drink." The body is a temple, not a refuge.

Page 77: Socho's Song Considered: Socho was a fifteenth-century *renga* poet and frequent visitor at Ikkyū Sōjun's little temple, Shuon-an, in the 1470s.

Page 80: Song of the Dream Garden: Re-visioned from Ikkyū Sōjun's celebrations of cunnilingus with his blind lover, Lady Mori, in *The Crazy Cloud Anthology*.

Page 83: After Clouds and Rain: "Cloud-rain" is a euphemism for sexual union. The term originated in a story by Sung Yu in the *Wen Hsuan* about a former Chinese emperor's tryst with the Goddess of Sorceress Mountain, and how it brought about his enlightenment.

Page 89: Ten Thousand Sutras: Re-visioned from "The Song of Zazen" by the great Rinzai master Hakuin (1685–1768), no doubt under the influence of Ikkyū's erotic koan-poems. *Samsara* is the cycle of birth-and-death. *Vivikta-dharma* is the Truth-of-Solitude central to the practice of zazen (*tso-ch'an* in Chinese, "deep sitting").

Page 92: Kannon: (See page 12 note, above). Te-shan (780–865) was a T'ang dynasty Ch'an (Zen) master renowned for severe teaching methods.

❖ *About the Author*

SAM HAMILL was born in 1942, probably somewhere in northern California. Abandoned in northern Utah during World War Two, he spent the war years in an orphanage before being adopted by a Utah farm family. Most of his adolescent years were spent in and out of jails and living on the streets. In his late teens, he enlisted in the U.S. Marine Corps in order to expunge his juvenile record and to see Japan. While serving on the island of Okinawa, he began studying Zen Buddhist literature and became a Conscientious Objector. During the 1960s, he was a civil rights activist and opposed the war in Viet Nam, campaigning for the California State Assembly in 1968 on a democratic-socialist platform. He attended Los Angeles Valley College and the University of California, Santa Barbara. He has served as editor at Copper Canyon Press since 1972, and lives with his partner, Tree Swenson, in a hand-built house near Port Townsend, Washington. He has taught in prisons, public schools, and universities, worked as an advocate for domestic violence programs, and has translated poetry from classical Chinese, Japanese, Latin, and Estonian. He has been awarded a National Endowment for the Arts Fellowship, a Guggenheim Fellowship, a Pacific Northwest Booksellers Award, the Japan-U.S. Fellowship, and the Pushcart Prize. Broken Moon Press will publish his literary essays, *A Poet's Work: The Other Side of Poetry,* in 1990.

Design by Tree Swenson.

The type is Perpetua, designed by Eric Gill. Composition by
The Typeworks, Vancouver, British Columbia.

Printed on acid-free paper and Smyth sewn in signatures by
Malloy Lithographing, Inc., Ann Arbor, Michigan.